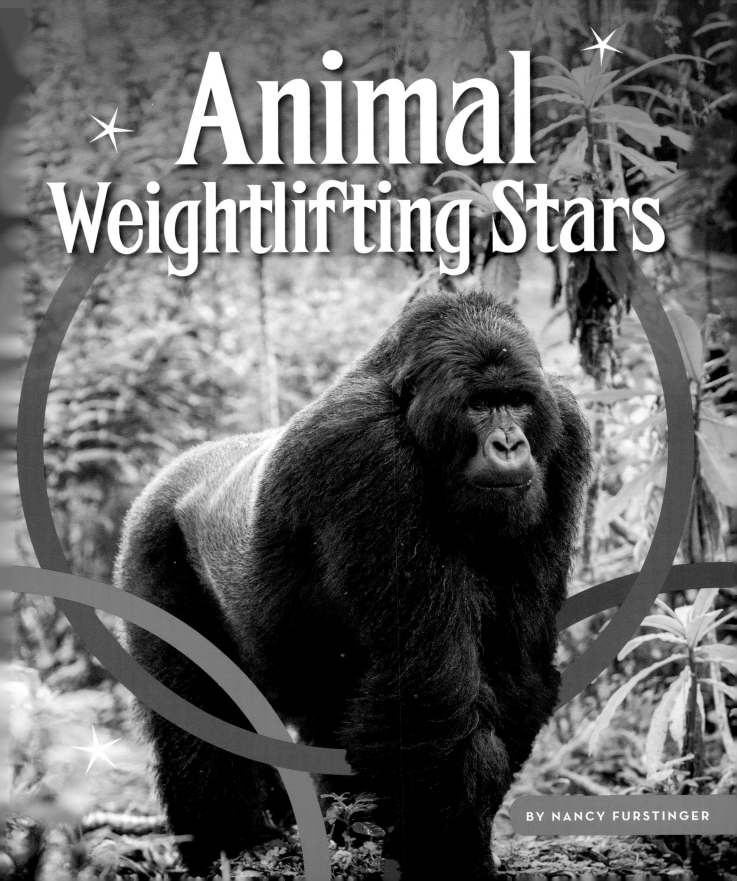

# Animal
# Weightlifting Stars

BY NANCY FURSTINGER

**The Child's World®**
childsworld.com

Published by The Child's World®
1980 Lookout Drive • Mankato, MN 56003-1705
800-599-READ • www.childsworld.com

Photographs ©: Wolfgang Kaehler/LightRocket/Getty Images,
cover, 1; Brian Kushner/Alamy, 5; Shutterstock Images, 6, 15;
Harry How/Getty Images Sport/USOC/Getty Images, 7;
Brian E. Kushner/iStockphoto, 9, 10, 21; Gudkov Andrey/
Shutterstock Images, 13, 20–21; Andy Rouse/Nature Picture
Library/Alamy, 14; iStockphoto, 17; blickwinkel/Alamy, 18, 20

ISBN 9781503820449
LCCN 2016960514

Printed in the United States of America
PA02341

## ABOUT THE AUTHOR

Nancy Furstinger has been speaking up for animals since she learned to talk. She is the author of nearly 100 books, including many on her favorite topic: animals! She started her writing career in third grade, when her class performed a play she wrote while recovering from chicken pox. Since then, Nancy has been a feature writer for a daily newspaper, a managing editor of trade and consumer magazines, and an editor at two children's book publishing houses.

# Contents

# CHAPTER 1

# Weightlifting Stars

The strongest animals on the planet come in all shapes and sizes. Some can lift, pull, push, or carry several times their body weight. These animals are amazing weightlifters. Which animals would win the gold, silver, and bronze medals if this were an Olympic competition?

Of course, animals don't lift barbells. Instead they use their strength for **defense** or to carry food. Some have strong arm muscles. Others have fierce beaks. Some have powerful legs. These animal bodybuilders have something in common with human weightlifters. They all need to eat well to be at peak strength.

*Eagles have strong claws that help them grip their food.*

*Both men and women compete in weightlifting.*

Strong animals have brute strength. This helps them survive in the wild. Could any of these animals outpower a human weightlifter?

Weightlifting is a test of strength and power. Athletes compete to press the heaviest weight overhead. Men and women weightlifters lift barbells loaded with weights at each end. Top athletes can lift up to three times their body weight.

Kendrick Farris has been weightlifting since the age of 12. This athlete has competed in three Olympic games. He set two American records at the 2008 Beijing games. Farris has lifted nearly four times his weight.

Farris is known for being a **vegan**. His all-plant diet gives him huge muscles. But these animal athletes have a lot of power as well.

**ATHLETE PROFILE**
**NAME:** Kendrick Farris
**BORN:** July 2, 1986, in Shreveport, Louisiana
**HEIGHT:** 5.7 feet (174 cm)
**WEIGHT:** 207 pounds (94 kg)
**RECORDS HELD:** 820 pounds (372 kg) total lift in 2013 Summer Universiade

# CHAPTER 2

# Mighty Eagle Talons

Everything about the bald eagle is powerful. Strong wings help them swoop down and then fly off. Fierce **talons** let eagles snatch prey, or food. Mighty leg muscles allow eagles to hang on to their catch.

Bald eagles have very strong grips. Huge fish can drag eagles beneath the water because the eagles aren't willing to let go. Some eagles tackle heavy salmon and then row to shore using their wings. These birds can seize and carry hefty prey nearly half their body weight.

**ANIMAL PROFILE**
**NAME:** Bald Eagle
**HEIGHT:** Up to 3.5 feet (107 cm)
**WINGSPAN:** 6 to 8 feet (1.8 to 2.4 m)
**WEIGHT:** 6.5 to 14 pounds (3 to 6 kg)
**LIFTING POWER:** 5 pounds (2 kg)

Bald eagles are found near large bodies of water.

*There are more than 60 species of eagles.*

Fish is the bald eagle's main prey. Sometimes they steal fish from other birds. Seabirds and small mammals are also on the menu. Others feed on rotting animal flesh.

Bald eagles live throughout North America. Half of North America's eagle population lives in Alaska. They prefer to nest in forests near lakes and rivers. Pairs build giant nests on the tops of trees.

Bald eagles were once endangered. But their numbers climbed back up when laws banned DDT, a chemical used to get rid of bugs. The chemical had worked its way up the food chain and started killing thousands of eagles. Now more than 10,000 pairs of eagles nest throughout the United States.

## Fun Fact

*Bald eagles have approximately 7,000 feathers. Their brown and white feathers molt in patches. Eagles lose feathers on their heads first. It takes approximately six months to replace their feathers. Young eagles have dark heads that turn white between ages four and five.*

# CHAPTER 3

# Super-Strong Gorillas

Mountain gorillas are the largest of the great apes. They live in groups called troops. The oldest and largest adult male is the troop leader and protector. This gorilla has earned the name silverback because a patch of silver hair covers his back.

The silverback displays his power when challenged. He stands on his back legs. He breaks and throws things, such as grass or branches. He bares his teeth. Then he charges the outsider.

**ANIMAL PROFILE**
**NAME:** Mountain Gorilla
**HEIGHT:** Up to 6 feet (183 cm)
**WEIGHT:** Up to 441 pounds (200 kg)
**LIFTING POWER:** 4,400 pounds (1,996 kg)

Gorillas walk on all fours, putting most of their weight on their knuckles.

Male gorillas pound their chests to show dominance.

## Fun Fact

*Gorillas use different sounds to communicate. They belch to stay in contact with their troop. They grumble to locate other gorillas. They roar and hoot while pounding their chests to show that they are powerful.*

These strong gorillas have powerful arms. They can lift ten times their body weight. Their arm muscles are larger than their leg muscles. Their arms are also longer than their legs. Gorillas have amazing upper-body strength.

*Gorilla troops can be as large as 30 gorillas.*

Mountain gorillas live in the forests of central and west Africa. There they forage for food. They live on a vegetarian diet of roots, leaves, stems, bark, and fruit.

Only approximately 700 mountain gorillas remain in the wild. People have moved into the gorillas' **habitat**. People also set wire snare traps to catch gorillas and other animals for food. Park rangers are clearing away these traps so gorillas don't disappear forever.

# CHAPTER 4

# Powerful Beetles

Horned dung beetles are powerful insects. In order to be strong, they need a healthy diet. The horned dung beetles get their name from the food they eat. They live on the liquid from animal waste, or poop.

Male horned dung beetles have huge horns. They turn into boxers when battling for a mate. A male will claim a tunnel that a female dug to lay eggs. He will guard the entrance. Sometimes a rival will try to enter the tunnel.

**ANIMAL PROFILE**
**NAME:** Horned Dung Beetle
**LENGTH:** Up to 2.5 inches (6 cm)
**WEIGHT:** 0.75 ounces (21 g)
**LIFTING POWER:** 53 pounds (24 kg)

*Sometimes dung beetles will fight over their dung piles.*

*Most dung beetles feast on dung from herbivores, or plant-eating animals.*

Then the males will lock their horns. They will try to push the other out.

There are three types of dung beetles. They are called rollers, tunnelers, and dwellers, depending on how they treat the dung. Some dung beetles roll large balls of dung. Then they eat the balls or lay their eggs in it.

Others dig the dung in tunnels. The last kind of dung beetle lives inside the dung. Dung beetles are native to Africa. Now they can be found on every continent except Antarctica.

Scientists wanted to find out how strong male horned dung beetles are. They glued thread to the rears of the males. They put the beetles into tunnels in a lab. Then they strung the thread across a pulley and tied it to a tiny bucket. They added drops of water to see how much weight each beetle could pull.

The results surprised the scientists. Horned dung beetles could pull 1,141 times their body weight. This is equal to a person dragging six double-decker buses full of people.

## Fun Fact

*Scientists performed another experiment with horned dung beetles to learn how they navigate. The beetles use the Milky Way. They plot a straight path by following the stars. What happens if they can't spot the stars? Scientists put tiny hats on the beetles to block out the stars. Then the beetles rolled around in circles.*

# CHAPTER 5

# The Award Ceremony

**GOLD MEDAL**
**Horned Dung Beetle**

**SILVER MEDAL**
**Mountain Gorilla**

The gold medal goes to the horned dung beetle!
This tiny insect is powerful for its size. Males can lift
54 pounds (24 kg). The silver medal goes to the mountain
gorilla. The silverback can lift 4,400 pounds (1,996 kg).
The bald eagle wins the bronze medal. Congratulations to
all these animal weightlifters!

**BRONZE MEDAL**
**Bald Eagle**

# Glossary

**defense** (dih-FENSS) Defense is something that is used to protect. The dung beetle has large horns that it uses as defense.

**habitat** (HAB-uh-tat) A habitat is the place where a plant or animal lives. Many mountain gorillas were killed off because people invaded their habitat.

**talons** (TAL-uhnz) Talons are sharp, hooked claws on the feet of birds of prey. The eagle has talons that help hold on to its prey.

**vegan** (VEE-guhn) A vegan does not eat anything that comes from an animal, including cheese and eggs. Kendrick Ferris builds muscle mass on his vegan diet.

# To Learn More

## In the Library

Bardoe, Cheryl. *Behold the Beautiful Dung Beetle.*
Watertown, MA: Charlesbridge, 2014.

George, Jean Craighead. *The Eagles Are Back.*
New York, NY: Dial Books for Young Readers, 2013.

Nichols, Michael. *Face to Face with Gorillas.* Washington, DC:
National Geographic Children's Books, 2009.

## On the Web

Visit our Web site for links about animals that
lift heavy amounts: **childsworld.com/links**

Note to Parents, Teachers, and Librarians: We routinely verify our
Web links to make sure they are safe and active sites.
So encourage your readers to check them out!

# Index